IRONMAN

IRON MAN VOL. 3: THE SECRET ORIGIN OF TONY STARK BOOK 2. Contains material originally published in magazine form as IRON MAN #12-17. First printing 2014. ISBN# 978-0-7851-6667-2. Published by MARVEL WORLDWIDE, INC., a subsidiary of MARVEL ENTERTAINMENT, LLC. OFFICE OF PUBLICATION: 135 West 50th Street, New York, NY 10020. Copyright © 2013 and 2014 Marvel Characters, Inc. All rights reserved. All characters featured in this issue and the distinctive names and likenesses thereof, and all related indicia are trademarks of Marvel Characters, Inc. No similarity between any of the names, characters, persons, and/or institutions in this magazine with those of any living or dead person or institution is intended, and any such similarity which may exist is purely coincidental. **Printed in the U.S.A.** ALAN FINE, EVP - Office of the President, Marvel Worldwide, Inc. and EVP & CMO Marvel Characters B.V.; DAN BUCKLEY, Publisher & President - Print, Animation & Digital Divisions; JOE QUESADA, Chief Creative Officer; TOM BREVOORT, SVP of Publishing; DAVID BOGART, SVP of Operations & Procurement, Publishing; C.B. CEBULSKI, SVP of Creator & Content Development; DAVID GABRIEL, SVP Print, Sales & Marketing; JIM O'KEEFE, VP of Operations & Logistics; DAN CARR, Executive Director of Publishing Technology; SUSAN CRESPI, Editorial Operations Manager; ALEX MORALES, Publishing Operations Manager; STAN LEE, Chairman Emeritus. For information regarding advertising in Marvel Comics or on Marvel.com, please contact Niza Disla, Director of Marvel Partnerships, at ndisla@marvel.com. For Marvel subscription inquiries, please call 800-217-9158. **Manufactured between 6/13/2014 and 7/21/2014 by R.R. DONNELLEY, INC., SALEM, VA, USA.**
LEGO and the Minifigure figurine are trademarks or copyrights of the LEGO Group of Companies. ©2013 The LEGO Group. Characters featured in particular decorations are not commercial products and might not be available for purchase.

10 9 8 7 6 5 4 3 2 1

Tony Stark is a technological visionary...a famous, wealthy and unparalled inventor. With the world's most advanced and powerful suit of armor, Stark valiantly protects the innocent as an invincible bright knight known as...

IRONMAN

KIERON GILLEN
WRITER

DALE EAGLESHAM
ARTIST, #12

GREG LAND
PENCILER, #13-14

JAY LEISTEN
INKER, #13-14

CARLO PAGULAYAN
PENCILER, #15-17

SCOTT HANNA
INKER, #15-17

GURU-eFX
COLORIST

VC'S JOE CARAMAGNA
LETTERER

GREG LAND & GURU-eFX
COVER ART, #12-16

PAUL RENAUD
COVER ART, #17

JON MOISAN & EMILY SHAW
ASSISTANT EDITORS

MARK PANICCIA
EDITOR

COLLECTION EDITOR: **JENNIFER GRÜNWALD**
ASSISTANT EDITOR: **SARAH BRUNSTAD**
ASSOCIATE MANAGING EDITOR: **ALEX STARBUCK**
EDITOR, SPECIAL PROJECTS: **MARK D. BEAZLEY**
SENIOR EDITOR, SPECIAL PROJECTS: **JEFF YOUNGQUIST**
SVP PRINT, SALES & MARKETING: **DAVID GABRIEL**
BOOK DESIGNER: **RODOLFO MURAGUCHI**

EDITOR IN CHIEF: **AXEL ALONSO**
CHIEF CREATIVE OFFICER: **JOE QUESADA**
PUBLISHER: **DAN BUCKLEY**
EXECUTIVE PRODUCER: **ALAN FINE**

Tony Stark is in deep space, currently the prisoner of the lunatic droid, Recorder 451, as more and more of his past is being revealed.

Years ago, after stealing 451 from a casino owned by the Greys, a group of alien mobsters, Howard and Maria Stark learn that the droid can save their ailing, unborn son. However, 451 reveals that Earth is on the precipice of becoming the next great cosmic power, and as such, is in danger of being wiped out by aggressive alien empires. 451 has made a promise to prevent that. In order to save the Earth, 451 proposes a deal that allows him to genetically alter their son to protect the Earth in the future.

Desperate, the Starks accepted the deal and the pregnancy went forward. But before the child could be born, the Greys came after their stolen property. Realizing that the child could never be safe as long as the Greys were still out there, 451 convinces Howard to take the fight to the aliens and eliminate them once and for all...

THE SECRET ORIGIN OF TONY STARK PART 3   12

ENOUGH, 451. STOP THE RECORDING. THAT'LL HAVE TO DO.

MORBID. A MESSAGE FROM BEYOND THE GRAVE, JUST IN CASE...

HELL, EVEN AT BEST, I'M GOING TO MISS THE BIRTH.

WHAT AM I GOING TO SAY? "SORRY I WASN'T THERE, SON. DADDY WAS OFF SHOOTING ALIENS." I CAN ALREADY SEE THE THERAPY BILL...

IT'S FOR A VERY GOOD REASON, MR. STARK. I'M SURE HE'LL UNDERSTAND.

AND, TO BE FRANK, IF HE DOESN'T THERE'S NO OTHER CHOICE.

WE HAVE TO ACT IMMEDIATELY. IF THE GREYS LEAK HIS EXISTENCE OFF-PLANET, YOUR FAMILY WILL NEVER KNOW PEACE.

OR, INDEED, FURTHER LIFE.

THE NURSE IS HERE, MARIA, I'VE GOT TO...

I KNOW. I KNOW. I KNOW.

HOWARD, JUST COME BACK.

"HEY, GUYS. IT'S HOWARD. GUESS WHAT? I'M GLAD I PAID YOU ALL TO STAY WITHIN SPRINTING DISTANCE OF VEGAS..."

NESSA
THE KITTEN..,

THAT'LL FORCE EVERYONE OUT OF THE BUILDING.

AND NOW WE HAVE OUR PRIVACY...

BUT, SIR. THE FIRE SERVICES! THE POLICE!

DON'T WORRY YOUR SHINY LITTLE HEAD.

THE MAYOR'S OFFICE.

GENTLEMEN, I KNOW IT'S LATE, BUT HERE'S AREA 52'S PAPERWORK FOR TONIGHT'S DISPLAY, AND A LITTLE *EXTRA* PAPER TO EXPEDITE THE PROCESS.

IT'S A SHOW. AN ORSON-WELLES-DOES-WAR-OF-THE-WORLDS HOAX. WE'VE GOT A ROBOT, EXPLOSIONS...

...AND FOR THE FINALE...

"...A WONDERFUL, COMPLETELY SAFE AND ENTIRELY FAKE UFO!"

I'M IMPRESSED, MR. STARK.

BE IMPRESSED AT NESSA. SHE'S THE BEST LIAR I KNOW.

LET'S MOVE.

SIR. I KNOW WHAT YOU MUST FEEL LIKE, BUT YOU MUST TRY TO REMEMBER WHAT YOU'LL HAVE ACHIEVED HERE.

IT'S A MAGICAL THING.

YEAH, MAYBE.

WE HAD A KID.

I... SHOULD SAY THANK YOU.

AS SHOULD I. NO ONE ELSE WILL. OUTSIDE OF US, NO ONE WILL EVER KNOW EXACTLY WHAT WE'VE DONE FOR THE EARTH.

IF ALL GOES WELL, WE WILL NEVER MEET AGAIN.

YOU SAID IT, YOU FREAKY CRAZY ROBOT.

THAT I AM, SIR.

MARIA? IS HE... OKAY?

OH, NO.

HE'S
WONDERFUL.

WHAT
DO WE DO
NOW?

DEEP SPACE, PRESENT DAY.

NO ONE WOULD KNOW THE FULL STORY, APART FROM YOUR PARENTS AND ME.

AND YOU DID EVERYTHING I COULD HAVE EVER HOPED FOR...

I CAN UNDERSTAND THAT YOU'RE ANGRY, BUT SURELY YOU MUST SEE THE NECESSITY?

SHUT UP.

"YOU'RE NOT MY FATHER, 451!"

STOP THE PETULANT MR. STARK, P.E.P.P.E.R.

WE HAVE MATTERS TO DISCUSS.

YES... SIR.

SORRY, TONY.

I PREPARED YOU. YOU PREPARED THE EARTH. BUT THE NEXT STEP IS MORE IMPORTANT.

NOT JUST TO SURVIVE, BUT TO PROSPER, TO PREPARE TO EXPAND...

SO, WHAT'S THE TWIST, YOU METAL FREAK?

WHAT DIDN'T YOU TELL MY PARENTS?

P.E.P.P.E.R., ARE YOU **SURE** YOU CAN'T REPULSOR-BLAST HIM?

NO CAN DO, TONY.

EARTH CAN STAND AGAINST ITS FOES...BUT IT NEEDS SOMETHING TO MAKE ITS FOES NEVER DREAM OF RAISING A FIST.

EARTH NEEDS A NUCLEAR DETERRENT.

EARTH **HAS** A NUCLEAR DETERRENT. IT ALSO HAS THOR.

ON THE SCALE I'M TALKING ABOUT, NUCLEAR WEAPONS OR EVEN THOR AREN'T MUCH OF A DETERRENT, MR. STARK.

A LONG TIME AGO, WHEN TIME WAS YOUNG, THERE WAS A WAR BETWEEN THE OLD POWERS OF THE COSMOS AND THOSE WHO WOULD DEPOSE THEM.

IN THE WAR AGAINST THE CELESTIALS, THE UPSTART FACTION MADE... CERTAIN WEAPONS.

I LOCATED ONE IN A STATE OF DISREPAIR. OVER THE PAST FEW HUNDRED YEARS, I'VE BEEN TRYING TO REACTIVATE IT. I GATHERED MISSING PIECES FROM DOZENS OF WORLDS.

EVENTUALLY, I ONLY NEEDED TWO THINGS...

THE HEART OF THE VOLDI...

AND ME, RIGHT?

CORRECT, MR. STARK.

I NEEDED A PILOT.

A PILOT FOR **WHAT**?

FOR THIS, MR. STARK.

ALMOST AS IF SOMETHING WAS NAGGING AWAY AT YOUR SUBCONSCIOUS...

I DON'T THINK LOOKING LIKE A BACKUP DANCER AT A DAZZLER GIG IS GOING TO FRIGHTEN THE SKRULLS INTO SUBSERVIENCE.

I ADMIT, I WASN'T EXPECTING IT AS A SIDE-EFFECTS OF THE IMPLANTS, BUT IT'S EVER-SO NEAT.

DIDN'T YOU EVER WONDER WHY YOU WERE SO OBSESSED WITH EXOSKELETONS?

ACTUALLY, MAYBE THAT WOULD.

LOOK CLOSER, MR. STARK.

25,000 feet

THAT THING'S NEARLY FIVE MILES TALL.

YOUR CREDITS HAVE BEEN SAFELY DEPOSITED IN OUR OMEGA-SECURITY VAULT, MR. DEATH'S HEAD.

AND MAY I SAY, THAT'S A *FINE* SCORE YOU'VE BROUGHT IN.

IS THERE ANYTHING ELSE I CAN DO FOR YOU TODAY, SIR?

NO, I'M GOOD. I...

PURELY AS A MATTER OF CURIOSITY, ARE THERE ANY OUTSTANDING BOUNTIES FOR A RECORDER?

WHAT KIND OF RECORDER, SIR?

RIGELLIAN.

OH YES! A FEW CENTURIES OLD, NOW, BUT THERE'S A REWARD FOR A ROGUE RIGELLIAN RECORDER THAT'S STILL UNCLAIMED.

WHAT DID HE DO?

HE SOMEHOW DOWNLOADED THE ENTIRE RIGELLIAN DATABASE INTO HIMSELF AND THEN DELETED PARTS OF THE MAIN ARCHIVE.

HE TOOK THE BACKUPS TOO. NO ONE HAS ANY IDEA WHAT WAS IN THERE.

A MISSING APPLIANCE AND A LITTLE LOST DATA.

CAN'T BE MUCH OF A REWARD, YES?

THIS IS THE FIGURE, SIR.

IS THERE A BUG IN YOUR DISPLAY OR...

NO BUG.

THAT'S AN EXCITING NUMBER OF ZEROES.

SO... YOU'VE SEEN HIM?

NO. MOST DEFINITELY NOT. IF I DID, I'D CERTAINLY SHARE THE NEWS WITH OTHER INTERESTED PARTIES, YES?

THERE'S ENOUGH FOR EVERYONE.

DAMMIT.

YOU ARE A FIRST-RATE FREELANCE PEACE-KEEPING AGENT, THIRD-RATE BUSINESS-BOT.

WHY DO YOU ALWAYS SKIP DUE DILIGENCE?

"NEARLY THERE, MR. STARK."

DEEP
SPACE.

IT'S AN M-BANKS CLASS ORBITAL BODY. BASICALLY A DYSON SPHERE AROUND A STABILIZED MICRO-STAR.

...A *COMPLETE* DYSON SPHERE. A STAR *ENTIRELY* SURROUNDED BY AN ARTIFICIAL STRUCTURE.

THE RESOURCES REQUIRED...

ASTRONOMICAL.

MR. STARK: ITS ARCHITECTS FOUGHT THE CELESTIALS FOR DOMINION OF ALL EXISTENCE AT THE BEGINNING OF TIME.

THE ASPIRANTS WERE NEVER THE TYPE TO THINK SMALL.

THE GODKILLER.

HOW DID YOU FIND THIS THING?

FOLLOWED THE CLUES. THE RIGELLIANS LOVE KNOWLEDGE, BUT THEY DON'T THINK ABOUT ITS APPLICATION. OR EVEN LOOK FOR PATTERNS, PARTICULARLY.

SUFFICIENT INFORMATION IS A TREASURE MAP, IF YOU APPROACH IT IN THE RIGHT MANNER. AND IT LED ME TO THE GODKILLER...

"THIS WAS THE FINAL BATTLE OF THE CELESTIAL WAR. THE ASPIRANTS WERE DESPERATE. THE CELESTIALS WERE TOO. THE GODKILLER TURNED THE BATTLE. SADLY, AS TIME WOULD TELL, IT FAILED TO WIN THEM THE WAR.

AS YOU CAN SEE, THE CONFLICT WAS...

HORRIBLE.

BEYOND ALL BELIEF, SIR.

AS A LINGUISTIC NOTE, IN THEIR LANGUAGE THE WORD "ASPIRANT" WAS IDENTICAL IN MEANING TO "TYRANT".

YOU ACTUALLY THINK YOU'RE ON OUR SIDE.

YOU JUST DON'T TRUST US TO DO THE JOB.

PRECISELY.

YOU COULD WASTE THE CHANCE, AND EVERYTHING I'VE DONE WILL BE FOR NAUGHT.

CAN'T RISK THAT, MR. STARK.

YES, THAT'S RIGHT, P.E.P.P.E.R., RIGHT THERE...

CONTROL ME, BUT DON'T PATRONIZE ME.

WELL DONE, 451. YOU MAY HAVE EXTERMINATED AN ENTIRE WORLD, BUT YOU'VE GAINED A LAVA LAMP.

PLEASE, MR. STARK. LET ME DEMONSTRATE...

GODKILLER: ACTIVATE...

DEATH'S HEAD! HE'S GOT ACCESS TO ALL MY SUIT'S ABILITIES, REMEMBER. YOU NEED TO--

HMM. PROBLEM, YES?

PROBLEM SOLVED!

THE SECRET ORIGIN OF TONY STARK:

TONY, I'M COMPROMISED. IF YOU DON'T DO SOMETHING, 451 WILL GO ALL GEPPETTO ON ME. I DON'T WANT TO BE A LITTLE WOODEN GIRL.

I--

DON'T PANIC, P.E.P.P.E.R., IT'S GOING TO BE OKAY.

SHUT DOWN.

LEAVE THE SUIT ON DUMB RESPONSE.

I MOVE, IT MOVES.

HE HACKS A.I.s AND COMPLICATED SYSTEMS?

WE'LL MAKE THE SYSTEM LESS COMPLICATED.

I GET IT. BE MORE LIKE A MACHINE, LESS LIKE A COMPUTER.

IF YOU SHORT-CIRCUIT THE WEAPONS YOU MAY BE ABLE TO GET A FEW SHOTS, TONY. MAKE THEM COUNT.

DON'T DO ANYTHING STUPID WHEN I'M GONE.

BE CAREFUL.

I'LL MISS YOU.

WAKE UP, DEATH'S HEAD.

YOU NOW HAVE THE FOLLOWING OPERATIONAL PARAMETERS...

NO AGGRESSIVE ACTIONS AGAINST ME.

FULFILL ALL SPECIFIED OBJECTIVES.

YOU WILL ACT ACCORDING TO THIS, YES?

I REALLY *DON'T* LIKE YOU.

THAT'S A PERFECTLY REASONABLE POSITION TO TAKE, CONSIDERING.

NOW, IF YOU WILL...

HMM. THE LOCAL EQUIVALENT OF SERVICE ELEVATORS? MAYBE SAFER THAN THE MAIN SHAFT?

MAYBE.

NOW I JUST NEED TO WORK OUT WHAT THE HELL I CAN DO.

THERE HE IS, ROBOT DICTATOR.

PACIFY HIM.

AS GENTLY AS YOU'RE ABLE.

NOTHING PERSONAL, STARK.

FOOM

SO, HE'S PAYING YOU?

NO. MIND CONTROL. VERY ANNOYING.

THE ONLY "FREE" DEATH'S HEAD LIKES IS HIS *FREEDOM*.

I SAID THERE WAS NOTHING PERSONAL AGAINST *YOU*. CONSIDERABLE "PERSONAL" AGAINST 451, YES?

REGRET COMING HERE NOW. BUT THE ROBOT IS A LIBRARY OF KNOWLEDGE. NEAR INFINITE, APPARENTLY. PRICELESS.

DON'T CARE ABOUT PRICELESS. ONLY CARE ABOUT THE PRICE ITS CREATORS WOULD PAY TO GET IT BACK.

BET YOU'RE WONDERING HOW I FOUND THE GODKILLER?

TO BE HONEST, I WAS MORE WORRIED ABOUT HOW I'M GOING TO AVOID BEING STEPPED ON.

YOUR ARMORY, STARK.

I SET IT TO HOME IN ON YOUR SUIT. CAME STRAIGHT HERE.

LANDED IN THE MOUTH-BAY DOCK, YES?

MY ARMORY. HERE? THANK YOU.

SILENCE! DON'T *TALK* TO HIM.

NO MORE CHAT. GET HIM!

LEAVING YOU FREEDOM OF SPEECH WAS A MISTAKE.

THAT WAS ALWAYS MY PROBLEM...

"I OWE YOU."

LET ME GO!

DONE.

FOOL. YOU FOOL. YOU DIDN'T HAVE TO DIE.

THAT WASN'T NECESSARY.

"HARD TURN-- WHAT WAS--"

NEW DESTINATION? *TARGET?*

THAT'S... HOPE'S PUSTULE.

HE'S AIMED THE GODKILLER AT AN INHABITED WORLD.

I HAVE TO STOP IT.

THINK, MR. STARK. THINK.

"THERE'S *ONE* SURE WAY TO STOP THE GODKILLER, ISN'T THERE?"

"YES, YOU'VE TIME TO *TRY* TO DISABLE IT.

"IF YOU COULD REMOVE THE HEART OF THE VOLDI...

"BUT SADLY, YOU *CAN'T.*"

WHAT'S THE *SURE* WAY?

"THE PILOT COULD STOP IT. *YOU'RE* THE PILOT.

"ACCEPT YOUR DESTINY."

STEVE. THOR. EVERYONE ELSE.

DOWN TO YOU GUYS NOW.

YOU'LL STOP HIM.

YOU'LL STOP WHATEVER THIS TURNS ME INTO.

OH GREAT.

I'M REDUCED TO ACTUALLY HAVING FAITH IN GODS AND MY FELLOW MAN.

15 THE SECRET ORIGIN OF TONY STARK:
THE BEST OFFENSE PART 3

SURELY YOU'RE NOT WILLING TO LET THE EARTH DIE TO SAVE YOUR OWN SELFISH SELF?

YOU'LL BE A BETTER YOU WITH MY PROGRAMMING. PLEASE. *PLEASE.*

BECOME THE PILOT OF THE GODKILLER. UNLOCK THE TRUE POWER OF THIS WEAPON. EVEN WITH JUST ITS AUTOPILOT, IT CAN DESTROY WORLDS.

IMAGINE WHAT AN EMPIRE EARTH COULD HAVE IF IT WAS ACTUALLY *WORKING.* WITH YOU IN ITS COCKPIT.

AND IF YOU DON'T, I'VE COME PREPARED TO DRAG YOU THERE MYSELF.

IN MY NEAR INFINITE DATABASES, YOU CAN'T BE SURPRISED THERE'S SCHEMATICS OF WEAPONS I CAN CONSTRUCT...

AND SUFFICIENT NOVEL TECHNOLOGY IN THE GODKILLER FOR ME TO REPURPOSE INTO THE TASK...

I DON'T WANT TO DO THIS. DON'T WANT ANY OF THIS...

...BUT I MUST DO WHAT I HAVE TO.

THIS IS OVER.

JUPITER'S ORBIT.

"STOP THE GODKILLER NOW."

I'M SORRY. NOTHING HAS CHANGED, MR. STARK. I CAN'T FORCE YOU TO JOIN WITH THE MACHINE...BUT YOU HAVE TO DO IT YOURSELF. OR ELSE EARTH WILL DIE.

THE PLAN HAS TO SUCCEED.

YOU WANTED ME TO UNDERSTAND?

NOW IT'S YOUR TURN.

WATCH, 451. ANOTHER OF YOUR PRECIOUS INTERFACE STATIONS...

THIS ONE'S A BIO-TELEPATHY FIELD, RIGHT? IT SHOULD JUST ALIGN...NOW.

AND NOW I SHOULD BE INTERFACED, RIGHT?

AND NOTHING HAPPENS, 451!

GODKILLER: ACQUIRE GENETIC HOOKS.

REALIGN TELEPATHIC GRID TO PRESET PROGRAM C.

ᚱᛖᚨᛚᛁᚷᚾ ᚨᚷᚨᛁᚾ ᛏᛟᛟᛚ

I SAID, REALIGN TELEPATHIC GRID...TO PROGRAM...

I SAID...

ᚱᛖᚨᛚᛁᚷᚾ ᚨᚷᚨᛁᚾ ᛏᛟᛟᛚ

IT'S ALIGNED. IT'S...

IT DOESN'T WORK!

"BUT MY PLAN
WAS PERFECT.
IT WAS TRUE.
IT..."

I DON'T
CARE IF IT'S
TRUE!

IF IT'S
TRUE, YOU
MESSED UP,
451.

I
MISCALCULATED.

I...

FIVE
HUNDRED YEARS.
451,286,112. /-5
1.0 SENTIENTS.

THE ENDS
JUSTIFY THE
MEANS.

THERE WERE
NO ENDS. JUST THE
MEANS. MY MEANS
WERE MONSTROUS.
MY...

ONE SHOULD
NOT HAVE
ACTED.

ONE--

NO MATTER
WHAT REASONS
YOU HAVE FOR ACTING
LIKE ULTRON, YOU
DON'T ACT LIKE
ULTRON.

"LISTEN! YOU
DON'T GET TO
FREEZE
UP NOW!"

LEAVING THIS WEAPON OR YOURSELF IN EXISTENCE RISKS INCALCULABLE DISASTER. I WOULD DESTROY IT, IF I COULD, BUT THAT IS BEYOND ANYONE'S POWERS. INSTEAD, I MUST HIDE YOU BOTH AS BEST I CAN.

I'M SORRY, MR. STARK. I'M SORRY FOR ALL THIS. BUT YOU ARE ONE LIFE.

THERE MAY BE ONE WHO WORKS OUT WHAT MY ERROR WAS WITH YOU AND PROFITS FROM THAT.

EVEN THAT YOU *KNOW* OF ITS EXISTENCE MEANS YOU CANNOT ESCAPE.

451, LISTEN TO ME. DON'T DO THIS. THINK.

IT WOULD HAVE BEEN BETTER NEVER TO ACT.

IT WOULD BE BETTER TO HAVE NEVER EXISTED.

ONE MUST DELETE THE ERROR.

451! HOW DO WE GET OFF?! JUST DON'T MAKE ANOTHER MISTAKE.

TONY, IT'S NOT GOING TO WORK.

YEAH, I KNOW.

0.366

ARMORY!

YES, BOSS?

HOOK UP EVERY HACKING TOOL I HAVE TO 451.

THIRTY INTRUSION POINTS IN THREE SECONDS.

TONY, YOU'RE GOOD AT THIS--

THANKS, P.E.P.P.E.R., I KNOW.

YOU'RE VERY KIND.

BUT EVEN AT THIS RATE, IT'LL TAKE YOU A MONTH TO GET THROUGH.

HATE TO BREAK IT TO YOU, BUT WE DON'T HAVE A MONTH.

WE JUST DON'T HAVE THE TECH.

CATCH-22. THE TECH TO DO IT WOULD BE IN THAT DATABASE OF HIS. WE NEED TO BE INSIDE TO *GET* INSIDE.

WONDERFUL. I-- 451'S TECH...

0.519

NEW PLAN, P.E.P.P.E.R.

WE'VE GOT TO HUSTLE.

ZZZPPRRP!

TONY?

DEATH'S HEAD'S SHIP?

0.679

IT'S STRUCTURALLY STRONGER THAN THE ARMORY...

...BUT IT'S STILL NOT GOING TO BE ABLE TO PUNCH THROUGH THE GODKILLER'S SHIELD.

KRSH

TONY?

WHAT ARE YOU DOING?

0.701

START THE HACK AGAIN.

TONY, WE'VE LOST TIME. DISTORTIONS ARE REACHING CRITICAL LEVELS. WE'RE GOING TO END UP IN SOME CRAZY SUB-DIMENSION AND--

I'VE GOT A HUNCH.

REMEMBER DEATH'S HEAD'S STATE-OF-THE-ART ECM SUITE?

"REMEMBER WHEN I ASKED HIM ABOUT IT?"

WHERE DID YOU GET THEM FROM?

PROBABLY BEST IF YOU DIDN'T ASK QUESTIONS LIKE THAT, YES?

MAY ANSWER.

I THINK DEATH'S HEAD GOT HIS TECH FROM 451 AS PART OF THE PAYMENT FOR SELLING ME OUT.

AND IF IT'S A 451-LEVEL SYSTEM...

TONY... I'VE GOT THE ACCESS CODES.

THEN WHY ARE WE STILL HERE?

IT'S BEEN GOOD HAVING YOU WITH US.

HISTORIC AGE OF COOPERATION BETWEEN THE STARS AND BLAH-BLAH-BLAH.

HONORED TO BLAH WITH PETER BLAH AND THE GUARDIANS OF THE BLAH-BLAH.

TONY. YOU HAVEN'T EXACTLY BEEN TALKATIVE. I UNDERSTAND THAT... BUT BEFORE YOU GO, I HAVE TO ASK.

TWO WORLDS DEAD BECAUSE OF A ROGUE RIGELLIAN RECORDER? THAT'S AS HARD AS IT GETS. THAT MUCH KNOWLEDGE MISAPPLIED? MAKES ME SHIVER EVEN TO THINK ABOUT IT.

BUT IS THERE *ANYTHING* WE SHOULD KNOW ABOUT WHAT WENT DOWN WITH THE ROBOT?

BAR THE SHEER HORROR OF IT ALL? NOTHING UNUSUAL.

HE TRIED TO DRAG ME INTO HIS DIABOLICAL PLAN. HE FAILED. HE KILLED HIMSELF.

HE'S NOT A PROBLEM ANYMORE.

"THERE'S NOTHING ELSE YOU NEED TO KNOW."

TONY...

THIS IS PROBABLY A BAD IDEA.

YOU KNOW THAT, RIGHT?

P.E.P.P.E.R., I HAVE PLANS.

MAKING MY OWN MISTAKES NOW.

A SLICE OF PEPPERONI.

I'VE MISSED YOU SO MUCH, BEAUTIFUL.

NORMALITY. A TASTE OF NORMALITY, AT LAST. FINALLY GET TO TALK...

HEY, ROBO-P.E.P.P.E.R.? PUT ME THROUGH TO CLASSIC HUMAN-FLAVOR PEPPER.

HEY, MS. POTTS. GUESS WHO'S HOME?

TONY?

THANK GOD!

GET TO L.A., QUICK AS YOU CAN.

WHAT'S WRONG?

CAN'T TALK OVER A LINE. SOMEONE MAY HEAR.

PEPPER, CAN'T YOU--

NO TIME!

"JUST MOVE, YOU IDIOT! I'LL MEET YOU AT YOUR PLACE!"

PEPPER, WHAT'S WRONG?

IS IT ANYTHING TO DO WITH A ROBOT? BECAUSE IF IT IS, WE--

THANK GOD YOU'RE HERE, TONY.

THIS WAY.

QUICKLY.

OH GOD.

FOR THE RECORD, YOU ARE EVIL.

LEAVING EARTH TO DODGE AN AWKWARD BIRTHDAY, TONY? PRETTY DESPERATE, EVEN FOR YOU. WASN'T GOING TO LET YOU GET AWAY WITH THAT.

I'VE NEVER LIKED BIRTHDAYS. ALWAYS FEEL OFF AROUND THEM...

HOWEVER, DESPITE YOUR CRUELTY, I APPRECIATE THE DIPLOMACY WITH THE CANDLES.

TACT BORN OF YEARS OF PRACTICE DEALING WITH A HORRIBLE BOSS.

DID YOU HAVE EVERYONE ON SOME KIND OF TONY SURPRISE PARTY ALERT?

OH YES. DISAPPEARING INTO SPACE JUST GAVE ME MORE TIME TO PLAN. NO ONE ESCAPES PEPPER.

NO ONE!

IF SUPER VILLAINS WERE HALF AS GOOD AS YOU, EARTH WOULD BE IN TROUBLE.

ACTUALLY, SPEAKING OF SUPER VILLAINS I'V--

YOU SAY THE SWEETEST THINGS.

AND SURPRISES ARE FUN.

TONY, THIS IS MARC.

AND MARC IS... YOUR BOYFRIEND?

NO.

≶KOFF≶

NOW, TONY.

SAY CONGRATULATIONS AND DON'T BE WEIRD WITH MY FIANCE.

CONGRATULATIONS!

AND PEPPER?

I'M *DEEPLY* OFFENDED. YOU THINK I'LL BE WEIRD ABOUT THIS?

WHAT KIND OF FRIEND DO YOU THINK I AM?

P.E.P.P.E.R., OPEN THE FAMILY VAULT. I'VE GOT A NAGGING SUSPICION.

YOU KNOW, MY NAMESAKE DID TELL YOU NOT TO BE WEIRD ABOUT MARC.

IT'S NOT ABOUT MARC. IT'S ABOUT 451'S STORY.

THE PARANOID AND OVER-PROTECTIVE FRIEND ROUTINE WILL WAIT.

TONY, YOU PROMISED.

AND SHE BELIEVED ME. IT'S ALMOST AS IF SHE DOESN'T KNOW ME AT ALL.

WHO KNOWS...

"...MAYBE SHE DOESN'T."

TONY. THIS IS A PARTY. FOR YOU.

THIS IS NOT A POLITE TIME FOR PAPERWORK.

TONY?

MOM, DAD...MARIA, HOWARD...WHAT WERE YOU THINKING?

MARC, WHAT'S THAT YOU'RE DRINKING?

SOMETHING RED, WINE-LIKE AND EXPENSIVE.

GOOD CALL.

A VERY GOOD CALL.

PARTY CANCELLED.

I HAVE TO GO.

YOU'RE SCARING ME.

TONY, WHAT'S GOING ON?

17 THE SECRET ORIGIN OF TONY STARK CONCLUSION

"WE TOOK 451'S DEAL. A CURE FOR A DYING BOY IN EXCHANGE FOR LETTING THE ROBOT TURN HIM INTO SOME KIND OF TECHNOLOGICAL MESSIAH..."

"...AND I'D WATCH EVERY STEP OF THE WAY.

AWAY FROM MARIA AND THE DAMN ROBOT AT 'WORK,' I OBSESSED."

OKAY, OKAY.

THAT'S ALL OF THE LEONARDO ASSEMBLY...

...AND THAT'S IT.

COMPUTER. REMOVE WHAT I'VE MAPPED.

THAT SHOULD BE *EVERYTHING* THAT 451 WAS GOING TO ADD TO THE KID...

HIGHLIGHT ANY UNKNOWN VECTORS.

WHAT THE HELL IS *THAT?*

"WE HAD SUSPECTED.

"NOW I KNEW."

KLCK

MARIA?

IF 451 EVER FOUND OUT...

WE HAVE TO KEEP HIM SECRET, DON'T WE?

"SHE WAS RIGHT, TONY. SHE ALWAYS WAS."

"WE CRIED MOST THE NIGHT AND WHEN THE MORNING CAME, WE STARTED WORK."

"WE HAD TO HIDE THE BABY, AND 451 COULDN'T KNOW..."

TAP TAP TAP TAP

FOR THE RECORD, I'D HAVE WORKED IT OUT A DECADE AGO. WHAT KEPT YOU, TONY?

I...

SOMETHING MADE ME...START THINKING...BUT I... PUT IT OFF. I DUG INTO THE FAMILY RECORDS. READ BETWEEN THE LINES AND...

OH, HELL, NOW I'M HERE.

WHAT KEPT ME? BEEN BUSY, I GUESS.

TONY. TAKE YOUR TIME.

WE'VE GOT A LOT TO TALK ABOUT.

WHERE DO YOU WANT TO START?

SO...

...YOU TYPE QUICKLY.

I'M SORRY, ARNO. I CAN'T *THINK* WHERE TO START, SO I JUST HIDE BEHIND JOKES.

YOU'RE TONY STARK. YOU'VE BEEN IN THE NEWS FOR EVERY DAY IN THE LAST DECADE, AND AT LEAST ONCE A WEEK BEFORE THAT. I KNEW WHAT TO EXPECT.

YEAH...I CAN BE A REAL WISECRACK SOMETIMES...

ARNO...I LISTENED TO DAD'S TAPE OVER AND OVER ON THE WAY HERE...

I'M STILL WRAPPING MY HEAD AROUND THE FACT THAT I'VE GOT A BROTHER WHO'S BEEN HIDDEN AWAY ALL THIS TIME.

BUT THERE'S SOMETHING ELSE DAD WAS TRYING TO SAY...

...

I AM ADOPTED.

THIS ISN'T HOW THEY'D HAVE WANTED YOU TO FIND OUT.

WELL, *ANOTHER* FINE EXAMPLE OF THEIR STERLING COMMUNICATION SKILLS.

I WAS JUST A DISTRACTION.

SOME KID THEY RAISED TO MAKE SURE THAT THE ROBOT NEVER REALIZED THE TRUTH ABOUT THEIR *REAL* CHILD.

YOU *WERE* THEIR CHILD.

THEY WERE PROUD OF YOU. THEY LOVED YOU. THEY WERE... AMAZED BY WHAT YOU WERE.

THEY TALKED ABOUT YOU ALL THE TIME.

THAT'S GOOD.

THEY NEVER TALKED *TO* ME AT ALL.

YOU KNOW, IT DOES MAKE SOME THINGS MAKE SENSE.

I DID EVERYTHING TO TRY AND PLEASE HOWARD. I COULD SEE THAT PART OF HIM LOVED IT AND THE OTHER PART WAS... SCARED?

MAYBE HE THOUGHT 451 HAD OUTMANEUVERED HIM?

MAYBE IT WAS JUST BECAUSE HE KNEW I WASN'T HIS.

I'LL NEVER KNOW.

ARNO. I'M SORRY. I'M STANDING HERE AND YOU'RE LYING THERE AND I'M ALL WHINING LIKE A--

I'VE SPENT MY WHOLE LIFE KNOWING AND LIVING WITH THIS.

I KNOW MUCH MORE THAN YOU. ABOUT ME AND YOU. ALMOST EVERYTHING, ANYWAY.

YOUR BIOLOGICAL PARENTS ARE THE BIGGEST OF THOSE BLACK HOLES. I'M SORRY.

YOU KNOW, I WANT TO SAY SOMETHING TRITE.

"I KNOW WHO MY MOM AND POP WERE. THEY WERE THE PEOPLE WHO RAISED ME."

BUT I DON'T KNOW WHO THEY ARE.

I DON'T EVEN KNOW WHO I AM.

THE STORY THAT 451 TOLD ME...THAT I WAS DESIGNED TO DO EVERYTHING I'VE EVER DONE. THAT I WAS JUST A TOOL. I HATED THAT.

BEING ADOPTED...THIS IS NORMAL. THIS HAPPENS TO ALL KINDS OF PEOPLE.

IT SHOULD...

IT DOESN'T FEEL ANY DIFFERENT.

I CAN'T BELIEVE YOU NEVER CONTACTED ME.

I NEEDED TO STAY HIDDEN IN PLAIN SIGHT. IF 451 EVER SUSPECTED ANYTHING, GOD KNOWS WHAT HE'D HAVE DONE TO EARTH...

WHAT ABOUT A CURE?

IF IT WAS EASILY DONE, DON'T YOU THINK I'D HAVE DONE IT?

EVEN IF I HAD ALL *YOUR* RESOURCES, IT'D BE LIKE TRYING TO FIX YOUR IRON MAN SUIT WITH A STONE HAMMER.

SO I WAITED. IF I WAS FOUND? THAT'S ONE THING. BUT TO GO OUT THERE WHEN 451 COULD BE WAITING WAS TOO BIG A RISK F--

451 ISN'T A PROBLEM ANYMORE. HE'S GONE.

OH GOD. I'M FREE.

YES, ARNO. YOU'RE FREE.

TONY! I'VE SPENT MY LIFE HERE THINKING.

EARTH HAS PROBLEMS. I'D LIKE TO WORK ON SOLUTIONS.

I HAVE... IDEAS.

OH, I'M SURE YOU DO.

I'M NOT JOKING, TONY.

I'M NOT JOKING EITHER.

I *NEED* THIS. GIVE ME SOMETHING TO DO, ARNO, OR GIVE ME A BOTTLE.

BECAUSE REALLY?

And so ends the first year of Iron Man.

Back in issue one, I wrote that I didn't really have a destination in mind for the book. I suspect at this point, you may start to think I was lying to you.

Please. As if I'd do that to you. I only lie to editors.

When I wrote that intro, I had just finished the first arc, which I knew had to work as sort of a thematic overture of the whole run. I knew that when Tony took off for his journey into space, everything had to change. Tony was the Grail Knight, searching for knowledge. I knew whatever that would be, it'd be seismic. He'd come back changed forever.

I got the idea for the core origin in Gatwick airport, on the way to DICE comic con. I had an e-mail from Mark, talking about the possibilities for the third arc. He suggested that as it was the 50th anniversary, it'd be good to have something that harked back to the early days of Iron Man.

I thrust my phone in my pocket, immediately angry. Really?

As I've talked about previously, I had a different original plan for Iron Man – a sort of hard-science fiction Deadwood on the moon. When the idea of Tony joining the Guardians at the Marvel summit appeared, I realised two things...

I) This is clearly a great idea, and should be done. It's great for Tony, it's great for the Marvel Universe and it's great for the Guardians.

II) I can't do hard-science fiction stories at the same time. I need to set fire to all my plans.

I was right on both counts. In the end, the core idea of that run is happening in a poppier form over in the *Iron Man: Fatal Frontier* infinite comic, but back then, I just thought it was a sacrifice of the great altar of Iron Man's Better Future. Anyway — I'd done that, spent five issues setting up Tony going into space, and had just turned IRON MAN into a sister-book to Guardians of the Galaxy...

And now Mark seriously thought I was going to find a way to do a story about Earth fifty years ago?

I stomped along, snarling. How the hell are you going to do that? I'd have to do something like...

Turn Tony Into A Living Weapon Created By An Alien Conspiracy To Upgrade Earth For Nefarious Purposes.

I stumbled, a little shocked by the complete audacity of the idea. I shook my head. I couldn't do that.

I couldn't do that for lots of reasons. Marvel wouldn't let me, for one. But more importantly, it would annihilate the core of a character. Tony's belief he is a self-made man, who has built everything with his own two hands is completely core to him. It would destroy everything that made Tony who he is. I couldn't do that.

I took another few steps, and then stumbled again, almost laughing.

No, I couldn't do that. But that it was such an existential threat to Tony's existence made it perfect for a different sort of story. One of those core parts of drama is to remove the supporting pillars, and have a character face what they most fear. The idea of making Tony think he's just a machine — an Iron Man — and have to deal with who he is after you remove that egotistical heart struck me as full of potential. That there was obviously enough evidence to support a fairly convincing conspiracy theory was the other plus. It wasn't out of the blue. On some perverse level, it almost made sense.

Following that line of thinking let me strip away Tony's sense-of-self, and allowed him to have that odd moment in the Godkiller when he realised he'd rather be wiped out of existence than let anyone else suffer. Tony Stark is a living ego, but if it came to it, it's more important to save people. It's more important to be a hero. He's arguably the most flawed of the first-rank of Marvel's heroes, true. At least for me, that makes him all the more heroic.

I didn't know exactly that I'd end up there when I was walking through Gatwick, but I knew that I'd have to go somewhere like it.

So, if Tony wasn't this child, who was?

And Arno was there. Instantly.

I got on the phone to Mark just before boarding, and threw the molten core of the story at him, only occasionally glancing around to make sure no comic reader was eavesdropping. This felt like a story worth telling. Mark agreed. After a lot of battles, we were able to tell it.

I hope you feel the need to re-read the run at this point. There's been a lot building to this point that may now be clearer. And more importantly, I hope you feel the need to see what the Stark Brothers do next. It's been a long road to get here.

Thanks for joining me.

Kieron Gillen

#17 LEGO SKETCH VARIANT BY LEONEL CASTELLANI

MARVEL AUGMENTED REALITY (AR) ENHANCES AND CHANGES THE WAY YOU EXPERIENCE COMICS!

TO ACCESS THE FREE MARVEL AR CONTENT IN THIS BOOK*:

1. Locate the **AR** logo within the comic.
2. Go to Marvel.com/AR in your web browser.
3. Search by series title to find the corresponding AR.
4. Enjoy Marvel AR!

*All AR content that appears in this book has been archived and will be available only at Marvel.com/AR — no longer in the Marvel AR App. Content subject to change and availability.

IRON MAN AR INDEX